Enchantment of America
NEW ENGLAND COUNTRY
The Northeastern States

(One in a series of eight books)

The unique charm of New England is captured in simple text and many pictures.

The story of this intimate, beautiful group of states with its characteristic hard-rock mountains, tumbling waterfalls, lakes, rugged shore lines, forests, lowland river basins, is told through the perspective of its fascinating geology, its vivid history and its people.

The first people ranged through the region hunting the mammoth and other animals, thousands of years ago. Eventually they settled in villages where they raised corn and tapped the maple trees. Only through the friendliness of some of these Indians were the Pilgrims able to survive in a new land.

Here is New England today where the beauty of the country makes vacationing big business. With available water power everything from submarines to toothpicks is manufactured. It is a country rich in forests, minerals, marble, granite, fish and farmlands.

New England, America's earliest melting pot, has some of the oldest schools in the country and has contributed much to our heritage of art and culture.

The book ends with a separate section on each state with a picture map and specific information.

Enchantment of America

New England Country

THE NORTHEASTERN STATES

Connecticut • Maine • Massachusetts
New Hampshire • Rhode Island • Vermont

By Dorothy Wood

Illustrated by Tom Dunnington

CP CHILDRENS PRESS • CHICAGO

Educational Consultant for the
Enchantment of America Series:
Marilyn M. Spore, Laboratory School,
University of Chicago

Regional Consultant for
NEW ENGLAND COUNTRY:
Benjamin W. Labaree, Ph.D.,
Assistant Professor of History,
Harvard University

Library of Congress Catalog Card Number: 62-9074

Copyright, 1962, Childrens Press
Printed in the U.S.A.

6 7 8 9 10 11 12 13 14 15 16 17 18 19 20 21 22 23 24 25   R   75 74 73 72 71

Contents

The lay of the land—then and now

Location

New England is made up of Maine, Vermont, New Hampshire, Massachusetts, Connecticut, and Rhode Island. New England is the picturesque northeast corner of the United States.

New England is a country of hard-rock mountains, rocky hills, many deep, narrow valleys, and a few wide valleys of which the Connecticut Valley is the widest. Eastward, it is a country ruled by the sea.

Formation and Change

New England's most prominent land form, her mountains, heaved upward more than two hundred million years ago. When they had finished lifting their magnificent ranges of peaks above the land, the Appalachian Mountains reached northeast into Canada and southwest through Alabama.

They have been wearing down ever since. South of the New England region, many of the ranges were composed of soft sandstone and limestone and shale that wore down quickly. But New England had a generous share of hard rock, like granite and marble, and so the leveling process carried on by wind and water was slowed down.

Something else came to New England, however, that did not reach the ranges to the south. Ice came. Great sheets of it covered the land and pushed their way across it. As they moved, they carried soil and rock with them, scouring this load away from the solid rock foundations. Then the climate grew warmer. The ice melted and dropped the materials it carried.

Starting about two million years ago, this happened at least four times. In between the advances of the ice, there were warm periods of thousands of years when plants and animals came again. Then once more the ice locked the land. The end of the last advance of the ice was about 10,000 years ago, and it left the land much as it is today.

Mountains and Valleys

In New Hampshire's White Mountains in the Presidential Range, Mount Washington reaches 6,288 feet—much more than a mile high. Here, too, are the famous "notches," the narrow U-shaped valleys or passes cut by rivers of ice as they were pushed along by the advancing ice sheet. Franconia Notch and Crawford Notch are two of these; they served as passes through the mountains for the Indians and exploring white men.

At Franconia Notch is the giant rocky profile, that we know as "Old Man of the Mountain," or "The Great Stone Face." When we look at the face, which is granite, we are reminded that hard rock is the outstanding characteristic of these New England hills and mountains. Granite peaks and shoulders gleam in the sun above mantles of green forests.

Rocky, too, is the soil, with little fertility. In the grinding, scouring flow of the ice sheets and glaciers, the soil was carried away and left far to the south. Some of it was piled up in hills, or moraines, often blocking the flow of a river. The water held back formed a lake. Always, stone was intermixed with soil in the hills left behind by the ice.

10

The ice sheets left other marks as they melted and disappeared. Here and there the flow of a river was turned in a swirling motion as the waters poured away from the ice. Boulders caught in the current were carried around and around on the rocky bed of the stream, and they ground "potholes" in the solid rock. There is a big pothole near Franconia Notch, in the Big Basin. Another kind of hole was made in the moraines formed when the ice sheets dropped their load of earth and rocks. Big chunks of ice broke off and were deeply buried under rocks and mud. Later the chunks melted and the earth sank into the holes that were left, making the "kettle holes" that you can find in New England's hills today.

North of the White Mountains a high hill country blends into the great Appalachian Plateau of Maine. None of this is as high as the White Mountains, but it is an almost unending country of hills interlaced with deep ravines and valleys, with tumbling small streams and rivers and hundreds of beautiful lakes.

Over most of New England, there is a combination of mountain ranges and high, hilly plateau country. Vermont is almost entirely made up of the Green Mountains which run through the central section of the state from north to south. South of them in Massachusetts are the Berkshire Hills, which roll southward through Connecticut. Eastward, south of the White Mountains, a plateau highland of hills and lakes takes over in New Hampshire and follows south through Massachusetts, Connecticut, and Rhode Island.

Between these two broad general areas of highlands flows the great Connecticut River. It forms the boundary between New Hampshire and Vermont, with a wide part of its valley in each state, then it flows down the ever-broadening valley through Massachusetts and Connecticut to empty at last into Long Island Sound. This is the widest of all New England's valleys. But there are others; the broad Champlain Valley around Lake Champlain in northwestern Vermont, and the Merrimack Valley in southern New Hampshire are two of them.

New England Coastlands

Of the greatest importance in the lives of her people, New England's Coastal Plain is narrow compared with other parts of the Atlantic Coastal Plain. Much of it was apparently "lost at sea" in the days of the ice sheets.

The ice sheets were so vast and covered so much of the region that their weight on the land was tremendous. Under them, the land sank a little. As they melted, the land stayed low, especially along the seacoast, and water from the melting ice raised the level of the sea. So the sea moved in, drowning the Coastal Plain and deeply covering it for miles inland.

The coast of Maine today has hundreds of inlets and tiny bays deeply indenting it, forming rocky peninsulas that twist and turn on each other. Hundreds of islands are separated from the land altogether, clustering far out to sea. The Maine coast is a coast of drowned mountains, their tops forming the islands, high ridges forming the peninsulas. Wherever river valleys came down between the granite hills and mountains, the sea rushed in, making bays and inlets.

Now the sea pounds away at the hard cliffs of those mountains, wearing them away and making sand and gravel that piles up to form bars and beaches. But this is a slow process, so that even today the coast of Maine is made up much more of hard rock than it is of beaches.

The melting ice made big rivers which cut their way to the sea in deep valleys through the soft Coastal Plain—such rivers as the Penobscot and the Kennebec. When the land was drowned, the sea water rushed in along the river channels and made wide, deep bays. Today ocean-going ships can go to upriver cities like Bangor on the Penobscot and Augusta on the Kennebec because of the deep channels of the rivers.

Farther south, around Boston, another kind of land was lost to the sea. Here is the big Boston Basin, a lowland reaching far inland, with the Charles and Mystic rivers flowing through it and emptying into the sea. When the sea came in, it made a great harbor, deeply covering the lowlands and reaching back along the river valleys. Throughout this land were many "drumlins," low hills whose tops had been scoured round and smooth by the ice. The drumlins, too, were covered by the sea as it came in, but many of them only partially, so that today near Boston are many smooth, round islands made by the tops of the drumlins.

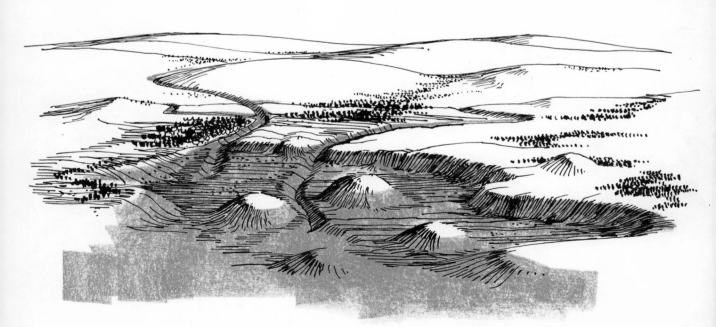

South of Boston the soft lands have been washed away by the sea until the great arm of Cape Cod has resulted. The arm was formed from soil and gravel that the ice sheet left; and the sea continues to pile up beaches and "hooks" in protected areas, to the north, to the south, and inside the long elbow of the cape, even while it pounds away at the outside face.

South of Cape Cod are two big islands that remain from the drowned Coastal Plain, Martha's Vineyard and Nantucket Island. Numerous smaller ones are near by. Block Island is another, lying farther west. They line up with Long Island in New York, also a part of the original Coastal Plain.

Rhode Island and Massachusetts share a group of drowned river mouths, forming another fine harbor north of Rhode Island Sound; Narragansett Bay is the biggest of the bays here, and Aquidneck Island and other large islands are an important part of the state of Rhode Island. Following westward, we find the Rhode Island and Connecticut shores deeply indented with group after group of inlets and barrier islands, and the deep mouths of the Thames and Connecticut and other rivers that make fine natural harbors.

15

Animals of the Ice Age

As the ice came down time after time from the north during the Ice Age it destroyed the forests and other plant life, and pushed the animals ahead of it. Many of them, like the deer and horses, moved much farther south and stayed until the ice receded, letting them come back. Others, such as the woolly mammoths, the musk oxen, and the caribou, lived sometimes within a mile or two of the ice and followed it north as it receded. Because of the woolly inner coats of their furry coverings, they were more comfortable in a cold climate than in a warm one.

So the animal life in this region was constantly changing. Just as the animals fled before the ice sheets, they traveled to a lesser degree with the summer and winter seasons. Other changes were going on, too. Many of these animals were king-sized specimens that we have never seen—great bears, and beavers as big as bears, huge buffalo and mammoths and mastodons, and enormous saber-toothed cats. These were beginning to die out in the Ice Age, and were gone long before our time. Others, like the camels and the early horses, migrated to Asia and were lost to this continent; the horses returned centuries later when they were brought by boat by the men of Europe.

Climate

Throughout New England there is what is called a "continental" climate, meaning that, for the most of the area, the climate is determined by location and land forms such as mountains and valleys. It is not greatly affected by the sea. Lying in northern latitudes which are cool to cold, and with high mountains, a continental climate in New England means one with long, cold winters and short, hot summers.

Add to "continental" the further quality of "humid," and you have a land of plentiful rainfall, lots of summer sunshine with warm days and cool nights, and lots of snow in winter.

Vermont, New Hampshire, and northern Maine are world-famous for their snowy winters. Here in the mountains the snow piles up to depths of many feet. Often a total of twelve to fifteen feet of snow falls through the winter. While a big snowfall and the "digging-out" afterward make headlines in almost any other part of America, Vermont, New Hampshire and Maine dig out from fall after fall of snow as a matter of normal winter living. Here are the country's first training grounds for skiing, tobogganing, and snow-shoeing. The mountains of these three states are filled with winter-sports areas that include some of the most popular and famous in the world. Here, too, are splendid forests, encouraged by plenty of moisture, in spite of a short growing season.

In the valleys, in the lowlands of Massachusetts, Connecticut, and Rhode Island, and all along the coast, the climate is more temperate,

with less snow and cold. Here the growing seasons are longer and wherever the soil permits, crops have a chance to grow and mature.

Along the sea the summer climate is so delightful that resorts line the seaside, filled with people who have come to enjoy the sunshine and ocean and to escape the inland heat.

Things to think about

How were New England's mountains formed?

How did the great ice sheets affect the physical features of this region?

Over thousands of years, what has happened to the soil and land formations along the Atlantic seaboard?

How were New England's coastal islands and peninsulas formed?

Describe the "continental" climate of New England.

People come to the northeast

The First People and Their Homes

About 25,000 years ago, the first people came to America. They crossed the Bering Strait from Asia, perhaps on a land bridge that was later submerged, or perhaps on a bridge of ice. A few of them came at first, probably following a herd of buffalo or a giant mammoth or some other prized game. More and more came until, over hundreds of years, there were many thousands of these small, brown, black-haired men and women and their families on this continent. They were the ancestors of our American Indians, and so we call them, too, "Indians."

They spread through this continent until they reached nearly every part of it, and South America as well. One big stream of people found their way into the Southwest. Others moved eastward and settled up and down the Mississippi and up and down the Ohio. Still others spread deep into the south and populated all the southeastern corner of the continent. Like the mammoths and the caribou, some stayed in the cold north and moved eastward, into the region of the Great Lakes and then farther east, into the New England country.

20

These people had three ways of getting food. They hunted, killing even the great mammoths by making a mass attack on one of them. They fished, spearing their fish with stone spearheads attached to wooden shafts. They gathered nuts and fruit from the forests. New England was a land of unlimited forests, rivers, lakes, and ocean, providing food for them.

One generation after another of these people, down through thousands of years, lived out their lives near the sea, moving inland to hunt. They lived in the river valleys, too, and around the lakes. They lived in little villages or hunting camps, and sometimes one of these grew, or several villages joined together, and made a tribe. As the years went by, the languages of the different tribes changed until each tribe spoke a language not understood by the others. Yet the tribes and their languages were related, and all were related to the great group of people from whom they came originally. We say that they belonged to the Algonquian language family, one of the largest of our Indian groups. The Indians of this group spread through the Middle West, along the middle Atlantic seacoast, all through New York, New England, and over much of Canada north of these areas.

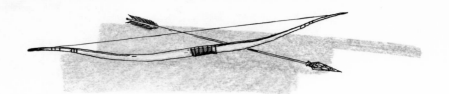

The Algonquians

Two of the Algonquian tribes in New England were the Penobscot and Passamaquoddy of Maine. In the southern half of New England were the Massachuset, Mohican, Nipmuck, Pequot, Wampanoag, Narragansett, and various others. The Algonquians were a peaceful people, engaged in their search for food and their battle against snow and ice which made food gathering difficult in winter. Some of them ranged westward into hunting grounds in Vermont and New Hampshire. Sometimes they were raided by the Iroquoians from the south and west, a powerful, warlike family who, like the Algonquians, were Eastern Woodland Indians and depended on the wealth of hunting grounds to feed their people.

The Algonquians built rounded shelters that we call "wigwams"—a word from their language. They bent poles to make the frame for a wigwam, then covered the frame with elm bark or, farther north, with birch bark, and often with skins in cold weather. A few tribes, one of them the Penobscot of Maine, built pointed tepees by stacking poles together in a cone and covering them with bark or skins.

Their dwellings were built near each other in little villages, and although one of these, or several together, might have a chief who advised the people, he had no real authority over them. The Indians were controlled by the gods of their religion, and followed leaders who won prominence by personal bravery and wisdom.

From traders who brought them seeds, or from southern tribes who drifted northward, the Algonquians of New England learned farming. They learned to grow squash and beans and pumpkins, and above all, corn. Corn was the miracle crop because they could eat it fresh, or they could dry it and pound it into meal which could be kept for winter and eaten then as bread. The stalks and leaves of the corn plant could be used for thatching the wigwams and for weaving mats. Cobs could be burned for fuel. So a large part of the Indian farming effort went into raising corn.

Still another kind of food came from the land. From the time the Indians learned to make strong containers from elm and birch bark, they tapped the maple trees early in the spring and caught the sap, just as it is done today in Vermont and New Hampshire. Using these same containers, they boiled the sap down and made sugar from it—another food they could store for winter. Still another food was the fish they caught and dried beneath the summer sun.

The Indians made various kinds of containers from bark. Some they could use for cooking, and others were boxlike and decorated and used to store food and personal belongings. They made baskets, too, and pottery, cruder than that of their neighbors to the south, but durable enough for widespread use.

Clothes were made from deerskin and the skin of other animals. In summer the men wore little, but in winter they wore leggings, skirts, and shirts that covered them warmly. Often their garments were heavily decorated with beading and fringes.

The Indians made their beads before the white man came, cutting them from bone and shells, and using porcupine quills and whole shells, too, for decoration. They made wampum beads from clam shells and used them as a kind of money, shaping and drilling them skillfully with tools of stone and bone. Each bead was cut from a thick part of the clam shell and carefully rounded. The hole was drilled parallel to the clam shell's wall instead of through it, so that the polished, pearly inside wall of the shell would be the outer part of the bead. The shell of a hardshell clam has a small spot of purple along the inside edge. So one or two beads from every shell of this kind would be purple. And since these purple beads were scarcest, they had the greatest value.

Great amounts of wampum went to the Iroquois to the south and west of the Algonquians. Sometimes the Iroquois traded for it, but more often they demanded it in tribute or simply took it as the spoils of war. They could not make it for themselves as they did not live where the clam shells were available. But they used it widely for trading, for sending messages, and for keeping records.

The Algonquians followed the forest trails, but wherever they could, they traveled by canoe. In the north, the canoes were usually of bark —light, strong birch bark whenever they could get it, or elm bark. The birch canoes were so light that one man could pick up his canoe and carry it from river to river or lake to lake. From Massachusetts south, the Indians often made dugout canoes, burning out the center of a large log and shaping it with stone adzes.

In winter, when they crossed the snow to hunt, the Indians had very fine snowshoes which we still copy today. They were made with a frame of green wood, bent in a long oval, and laced with a webbing of sinews made from animal hide.

Early Explorers

These were the Indians that Leif Ericson and his Norsemen found when they landed in about 1000 A.D. They explored briefly in a New England area that they called "Vinland" because of the many wild grapes growing there. John Cabot, too, sailed along the New England coast, landing at Cape Breton in Nova Scotia in 1497 and the next year sailing from Greenland down the shore of the Atlantic. Cabot was an Italian navigator but was employed by the British, and his explorations gave England claim to the whole New England region.

Yet by the time he arrived there, and increasingly in the years to come, the Spanish and the French were fishing up and down New England shores and trading with the Indians. It was a hundred years later, in 1614, before England's Captain John Smith sailed these shores and mapped them.

Meanwhile the Iroquois had spread northward from New York to the Canadian border, forcing the Algonquian tribes out of their hunting lands in Vermont and New Hampshire. Samuel de Champlain, French explorer and founder of Quebec, had made friends with the Algonquians in Canada. In 1609 he discovered and explored Lake Champlain at Vermont's northwestern corner, and he led an expedition against the Iroquois on behalf of the Algonquians and drove them south again. Thus he solidified Algonquian friendship for France and French colonists, but earned the undying hatred of the Iroquois.

27

The Pilgrims Come to Plymouth

In the fall of 1620 the English ship *Mayflower,* with about one hundred people aboard, landed at Cape Cod. Most of these people were "Pilgrims." They had traveled far in search of religious freedom, going from England to Holland, then coming to America. They had expected to set up a new colony in Virginia, but they were blown off course and were now many miles north of the Virginia settlements. Here they were on their own, with no form of established government. So before they left their ship, they drew up the "Mayflower Compact," containing laws that they agreed to abide by as colonists. The Mayflower Compact ranks as the first American instrument drawn up to serve as a constitution or set of governing principles.

The Pilgrims explored Cape Cod, the surrounding waters, and the nearby mainland. They chose a spot on the mainland to set up their colony and called it "Plymouth." The big rock that came to be known as "Plymouth Rock" is a symbol of their landing. You can see it at Plymouth today, as one of the most famous of New England landmarks.

The Pilgrims' first winter held many hardships that took the lives of half of them. But the Indians, headed by Massasoit, Squanto, and Samoset, gave them food through the winter and in the spring taught them to plant corn and other crops. By the time the second winter came, the Pilgrims had built substantial homes and had food stored away to see them through. And so, with the Indians as their guests, they celebrated the first Thanksgiving.

The Puritans

A new group of people soon came to the big bay farther north. They called it Massachusetts Bay, and their settlements, in the vicinity of the present Boston and Salem, were known as the Massachusetts Bay Colony. These people were the Puritans. They, too, had left England in search of a home where they could worship as they pleased. This colony grew rapidly, and by the middle of the century had many thousands of settlers.

But some of the settlers were dissatisfied with life in the Massachusetts Bay Colony. The Puritans insisted that everyone worship as they did, and the church and the government functioned together, so that only church members could vote. Roger Williams and Anne Hutchinson and many others believed that everyone had the right to worship as he pleased; Williams and others insisted that membership in a church should have nothing to do with the right to vote. So these people moved away from Massachusetts and set up colonies of their own, founding Rhode Island and Connecticut. Others went north and settled in what are now Maine, New Hampshire, and Vermont.

King Philip's War

As long as the great Chief Massasoit was alive, the Indians remained friendly to the white people. But Massasoit's son, King Philip, believed that unless the Indians fought for their lands, they would be wiped out. After Massasoit's death, he persuaded the Indians to fight, and in King Philip's War many colonists died before King Philip was killed and the Indians were defeated. King Philip's War lasted through 1675 and 1676.

The Colonies Grow

The strength of the New England settlements grew as many more colonists came to them. People in England and elsewhere in Europe were eager to escape from the oppression of religious restrictions, of almost constant war, and of a system that kept them from owning property. In the colonies they could own land and they could take part in governing themselves.

Massachusetts and other New England colonies were especially important for their town meetings, where men who owned property could vote. Others often attended these meetings and sometimes spoke, even though they could not vote. The town meetings carried on local government in the towns.

Each colony had an assembly elected by the voters to make laws for the whole colony. These assemblies were often under the authority of a governor appointed by the English king. But Rhode Island and Connecticut elected their own governors and were also entirely self-governing, their leaders fired with the spirit of new development and independence.

So the ability for self-government was growing throughout New England, and other abilities as well. The people had to learn to survive through the harsh winters of this northern country. They learned to supply their own food and shelter, using the materials of the land.

They had two great resources—fish and forests. A great fishing industry grew up along the sea. Great quantities of cod were caught in the Boston vicinity. The lobster catch was important all along the coast. Boats became more and more essential—fishing boats and sailing vessels to carry the catch to foreign markets. Whalers, too, were needed—stout ships that could sail the seas for many months at a time in search of whales for oil and whalebone.

The ship-building industry grew and prospered in the seacoast towns where there were fine natural harbors. Materials to build the ships came from the rich inland forests, and a prosperous lumbering business thrived wherever there were streams to run the sawmills.

Trade of all kinds developed as more and more colonial ships appeared on the seas; the colonies traded with each other and with many foreign countries, as well as with England. Fish and furs, iron and lumber were shipped, as well as woolen goods and other handmade products that the colonists turned out.

Merchants and ship-owners in the towns became wealthy, and the townspeople had better lives as markets increased for their services. Boston was a thriving city of shops and homes and bustling harbor —the largest in New England. Growing, too, were nearby Salem, Kennebunkport in Maine, Providence in Rhode Island, New Haven in Connecticut, and many others. The farmers probably gained least of all, for the soil was rocky and hard to work, and making a living from it was no easy thing. They built their homes themselves and made nearly everything in them. They worked hard to clear their land and farm it. But they owned the land, and they lived in freedom that they prized above everything else.

The French and Indian War

While the English colonies grew strong, French settlements were also growing north of them, along the St. Lawrence River. French explorers had traveled through the Great Lakes and down the Ohio and Mississippi rivers, and France was laying claim to all the interior of the continent. But England, too, claimed interior lands. Here was a vast country for settlement, and here, above all, was a rich fur trade with the Indians. The big rivers and the big lakes gave access to it.

So England and France went to war, from 1754 to 1763, to settle the matter, and the colonies fought for England. The Algonquian Indians sided with their French friends, and the Iroquois fought against the hated French, siding with the English.

One of the most important areas of the war was the Lake Champlain country in northwestern Vermont. The lake is only a short distance from the St. Lawrence River and it gave access to the Hudson River and all the country to the south. There were many battles and skirmishes fought on the lake and near it, centering around Fort Ticonderoga and Crown Point, on the New York side of the lake. Major Robert Rogers and his famed Rangers from New England took part in these battles.

The war was won by the English, and France lost her colonies on the North American continent, leaving the English in control.

Trouble with England

All up and down the Atlantic, the colonies were quarreling with their English governors and rebelling against taxes laid on them by the English Parliament. It was their right, they said, to levy taxes themselves. More and more trade restrictions, too, were imposed by England.

Virginia was up in arms against the dissolving of her House of Burgesses. The Sons of Liberty, with such patriots as John and Samuel Adams, James Otis, Paul Revere, John Hancock, and many others, became active in Massachusetts, in the rest of New England, and in the colonies to the south. Boston was a hotbed of rebellion; at the "Boston Tea Party" a group of her patriots dumped a cargo of English tea into Boston Harbor rather than pay tax on it.

So the English sent a fleet and an army to bottle up Boston and keep the back country under control. When the English army marched out of Boston to Concord and Lexington, intending to find and take any hidden arms and to capture John Hancock and Samuel Adams, Paul Revere made his famous ride ahead of the English soldiers to warn the two men and the countryside. The first shots of the Revolutionary War were fired at Lexington and Concord, and the Minutemen drove the British regulars back, empty handed, to their ships at Boston.

The War for Independence

The Second Continental Congress met in Philadelphia, attended by leaders from all the colonies, and voted to defend the colonies with an army led by George Washington. New England volunteers fought the Battle of Bunker Hill to free Boston from the British, and lost. But Washington shortly came to Cambridge, took charge of the Colonial army, renewed the siege of Boston, and drove the British out of the city. Several months later, on July 4, 1776, the Continental Congress voted in favor of the Declaration of Independence, and the colonies were in full-fledged war to win their independence from England.

In the next year of the war, Washington was driven out of New York but succeeded in holding New Jersey. Then, in September, 1777, he lost Philadelphia, and spent the terrible winter in Valley Forge. In New England many of the harbor cities suffered from bombardment by the British fleet. But in western New England, there was better news.

In the first days of the war, Ethan Allen and Seth Warner and their "Green Mountain Boys" from Vermont (which means "green mountain") had taken Fort Ticonderoga. General Burgoyne led a British army south from Canada, took the fort, and tried to proceed south through the Hudson Valley. He expected to meet a reinforcing army coming from the northwest, and another coming from New York. Neither of these reinforcements arrived, and Burgoyne suddenly found himself surrounded by the fighting men of New England. He was forced to surrender at Saratoga, New York. British attack on New England was ended.

This victory brought France into the war, since it then seemed to the French government that the colonies might be able to win. Although the war continued for four more years, it ended in the southern colonies when Washington, with the help of the French fleet, caught Cornwallis at Yorktown, Virginia, and forced him to surrender.

New States for a New Nation

In 1787 a Constitutional Convention was held in Philadelphia, attended by delegates from the states, and the Constitution of the United States was adopted. By 1790 it had been ratified by the four original states of New England—Massachusetts, Rhode Island, Connecticut, and New Hampshire. In 1791 Vermont became the fourteenth state, but it was not until 1820 that Maine separated from Massachusetts to become the twenty-third state of the Union.

As part of the young nation, New England's industries continued to grow. Her farming flourished in the wide river valleys, even though more and more hill farms were deserted as better land opened up in the West and people moved onto it. New people came from Europe but these were craftsmen and factory workers who stopped in the cities. So New England became a manufacturing center, and turned out everything from textiles and firearms to ships. Such craft products as Paul Revere's beautiful silver became famous around the world.

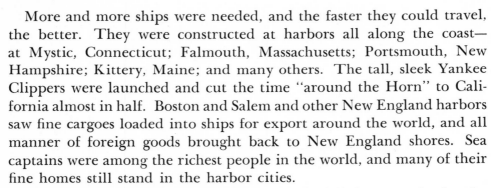

More and more ships were needed, and the faster they could travel, the better. They were constructed at harbors all along the coast—at Mystic, Connecticut; Falmouth, Massachusetts; Portsmouth, New Hampshire; Kittery, Maine; and many others. The tall, sleek Yankee Clippers were launched and cut the time "around the Horn" to California almost in half. Boston and Salem and other New England harbors saw fine cargoes loaded into ships for export around the world, and all manner of foreign goods brought back to New England shores. Sea captains were among the richest people in the world, and many of their fine homes still stand in the harbor cities.

This manufacturing and shipping world had little sympathy for the South when the question of slavery and secession arose. In Boston was founded the New England Anti-Slavery Society, which, as it spread through the north, became the American Anti-Slavery Society. Feeling was strong in New England against secession, and the region gave strong support, with soldiers and money, to the Union in the Civil War.

Afterward the development of industry continued, greatly advanced by invention of many kinds of machines to do work previously done by hand. With machines came development of steam and electrical power to operate them. This was the "Industrial Revolution" in America, a process that greatly affected New England by speeding up tremendously the manufacture of all kinds of materials and goods. In New England textiles were especially important; cotton goods of all kinds led the industries, and the biggest textile mills in the world were built to turn them out.

How did the New England Indians use the land, the forests, and the sea in their daily lives?

How did white settlement begin in New England?

Why did manufacturing and ship building prosper during New England's colonial days?

What natural resources did New England have which contributed to the colonies' manufacturing and industries? How were they used?

Describe the events which led to the eventual decision by the colonies to become an independent nation.

What part did the Indians play in the colonies' struggle for independence?

Life in New England today

New England — Manufacturing Empire

Name a product and the chances are that some of it, or something very like it, is manufactured in New England, especially if it's something with working parts that have to work exactly right. Clocks and watches? Look for them in Waltham, Massachusetts and Waterbury, Connecticut. Firearms? A dozen New England cities are famous for them; Springfield, Massachusetts, gave its name to the Springfield rifle. Missiles are manufactured in New England; atomic submarines are built at Groton, Connecticut. Toothpicks? Look in Maine for them and many other wood products, including ships and pleasure boats and paper. Vermont turns out marble and other building materials. New Hampshire makes maple sugar, pipe organs, ceramics. Submarines are built at the Naval base at Portsmouth.

These products are only a beginning. All over New England many things are manufactured in great quantities: cotton and woolen goods of all kinds, shoes and other leather goods, optical goods, tools, wood products, paper, paper pulp, and paper products, machinery, electrical supplies, typewriters and other office machines, sewing machines, silverware, rubber goods, and many, many other things. Various kinds of foods are processed; along the coast fish and seafood are frozen and canned.

What makes New England a manufacturing region? She must bring in most of her raw materials, importing them from all over the world. Much of her fuel—coal to burn, to keep her machinery moving—she brings in, too. There isn't much room for expansion.

Because of these drawbacks, New England has in recent years lost part of her textile industry. Many mills moved into the southern states, where they would be near the cotton supply. But the lost industry has been replaced by such products as missiles and electrical equipment, aircraft and airplane parts, and hundreds of other parts that go into all sorts of finished products. Many new research laboratories have come in, too. As new express highways have been built, plants for new manufacturing and research have been built alongside of them. Near Boston, for example, an express highway was built to by-pass the city. Industrial plants in carefully planned and beautifully landscaped parks grew up along the highway in such numbers that it is often called the "Electronic Highway."

Why is it that New England can turn out such a large proportion of the world's manufactured goods? There are several reasons. One is the tremendous supply of water power along her rivers. Another is her great harbors, allowing easy shipping. Still another is the fact that manufacturing people came early to New England, from all parts of Europe—people who were skilled in the special arts of making things. They made New England a manufacturing region, turning out with great skill all kinds of precision products.

Distances are short in New England, and railroads and truckers move materials to and from the harbors, carrying raw materials to the inland cities, and carrying their manufactured goods to the harbors. The lowlands are a network of railroads and fine highways, many of them expressways, which reach, too, into the mountains. New England's excellent transportation is one of the reasons why manufacturing is so successful there.

Moreover, the New England factories are near the great cities of New York, Philadelphia, Washington, and others. So they have ready, nearby markets for their wares.

Rivers Mean Power

In New England nearly every city is built on a river. Such rivers as the Connecticut, the Merrimack, the Kennebec, and the Penobscot have on their banks inland cities like Hartford, Springfield, Manchester, Augusta, and Bangor. It is no coincidence that such cities are manufacturing centers. The rivers all over New England rush down with great force from the mountains. There are many falls and rapids.

All this rushing water means power. In the early days of New England, the water was made to turn big wheels that turned the machinery of sawmills and factories. Today it operates the turbines of generators, changing water power to electricity, and so is a source of tremendous power for the factories' machines. Where power is to be had, industrial cities have grown.

Power is coming now from another source. The Yankee Atomic Electric Plant at Rowe, Massachusetts, turns atomic energy into electricity. The electricity made here is used in all the New England states.

Harbors Mean Shipping

At the mouths of many of the rivers, where they empty into the sea, are fine harbors. Here ocean-going ships come in, leave their cargoes of raw materials, and take away millions of pounds of manufactured products for other ports in the United States and foreign countries. Go to Boston, to Portland, to Portsmouth, to Providence, to New Haven, and you will see this shipping going on. Every state in New England has fine Atlantic Ocean harbors except Vermont—and even Vermont has an important port at Burlington, on Lake Champlain.

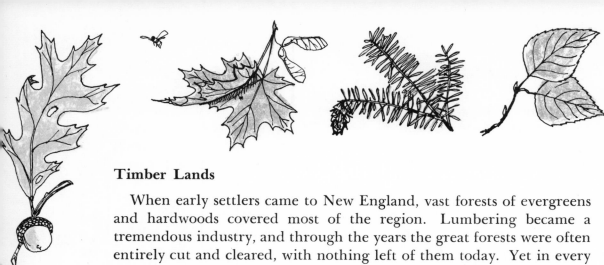

Timber Lands

When early settlers came to New England, vast forests of evergreens and hardwoods covered most of the region. Lumbering became a tremendous industry, and through the years the great forests were often entirely cut and cleared, with nothing left of them today. Yet in every New England state, at least a third of the area is wooded, and eighty-four per cent of New Hampshire is covered with splendid forests.

New Hampshire has spruce, fir, and white pine; birch, beech, maple, hemlock and oak. Maine is two-thirds forested, with white pine, spruce, balsam, fir, oak, hemlock, birch, beech, and maple. Vermont has sugar maple, hemlock, birch, and beech, with spruce and fir in the Green Mountains and white pine in the Connecticut Valley.

Extensive lumbering goes on in the forests, supplying wood for lumber and for the plants throughout New England that manufacture products of wood. Berlin, New Hampshire, for example, is in the middle of a lumbering area and has important paper and pulp mills. So do Augusta and Bangor, Maine, and many other New England towns and cities.

Vermont and New Hampshire lead in a world-famous by-product of the forests. Each spring, when the sap begins to run as the long winter comes to an end, it is extracted from the sugar maple trees, much as the Indians did it, and processed to make maple sugar and syrup. These tasty products are shipped all over the world from New England. So important is this industry in Vermont that the sugar maple is her state tree.

Quarries and Mines

When you start looking for minerals in New England, one of the first things you're likely to find is a granite quarry. Every New England state has granite, fine-grained and hard, known all over the country for its qualities as building stone. Barre, in Vermont, leads the United States as a producer of granite.

Vermont is a famous leader in the production of marble. From her quarries came the marble—white, red, blue, green—that went into many famous American buildings; these include the United States Senate Building in Washington, D. C., and the United Nations Building in New York.

Many other minerals come from New England. Some of the other building stones quarried there are slate and limestone, sandstone and basalt. The largest asbestos mines in the country are in northern Vermont. Feldspar and mica come from all the states, and all of them supply sand and gravel for building roads and clay for making bricks. In many places are found such minerals as titanium, copper, manganese, vanadium, and cobalt. Precious stones are found in widely scattered parts of the region—stones such as tourmaline and beryl and garnets.

Saltwater Fisheries

From earliest times, the fisheries of New England have been of major importance. Fishermen came to her shores before the colonists came. Today the lobster beds of Maine, the cod fisheries of Massachusetts, are known throughout the world.

Massachusetts leads the other states with her annual fish catch. Besides cod, she takes from the sea haddock and mackerel, halibut and herring, flounder, shad, bluefish, and millions of pounds of lobsters, oysters, and clams. These same fish and shellfish are taken all along the coast—in Maine, in Rhode Island and Connecticut. Boston, Gloucester, Portland and the big bays north of there in Maine, have fishing fleets coming in with their big catches of mackerel, herring, and dozens of other kinds of fish. Among many other kinds of seafood, Maine supplies most of the herring packed as sardines in this country. From Block Island, off the coast of Rhode Island, come large quantities of tuna.

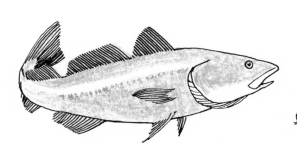

New England Farms

Plagued by poor soil, rocky hills, and a short growing season, New England still has some of the finest farms in the country. The broad Connecticut Valley, the Merrimack and other river valleys, the lowlands around Lake Champlain, and various other low, fairly level areas have rich soil and produce fine crops. Small farms are the rule, producing such crops as hay, corn, oats, and potatoes.

Maine is our first state in potato production, the northern part of the state taking the lead; and from this state come three-fourths of the blueberries in the United States.

In all of the states, apples and other fruit are important crops. Dairying and poultry-raising are part of the agriculture of every state and in Connecticut become major activities. Rhode Island's poultry is so important that a breed of chicken is named for the state—the Rhode Island Red; and from Massachusetts comes the name of the Plymouth Rock.

Connecticut is unique in the growing of fine tobacco under tent shade in the Connecticut Valley. Massachusetts' unique crop is cranberries, grown in great bogs on Cape Cod. The Cape Cod and Boston areas and the coastal plain of Rhode Island and Connecticut have many truck farms that send vegetables to city markets.

44

Visitors in New England

The New England states make up one of the greatest vacation areas of our country, and as a result, the tourist business in New England is "big" business. Millions of visitors go there every year for a wide variety of vacation recreation. They can motor and hike and camp in the forested mountains; they can rest in the sun in the beautiful, meadowed valleys; they can swim in ocean and lake, go boating and skiing on the water, and sun-bathe on the beaches. There are many kinds of enchantment in New England to attract visitors year after year. The money that they spend there is one of the region's chief sources of income.

New England does many things to attract vacationers. Wherever there is open water there are resorts where visitors can stay while they enjoy their vacations. They can rent boats and fishing equipment; they can camp in any of dozens of campgrounds in the state parks and forests.

Visitors are always interested in the old things of a region, and New England has been wise in preserving and restoring her historic spots—old homes, old inns, in fact, whole villages have been restored to look as they did in early times. The history of New England is one of its most important attractions to visitors.

The People

From the very beginning, the people of New England have been known as both industrious and independent. As we have seen, the first white people to live in New England were mostly English—people who came here with ideas of their own about religion and politics, and the will to live according to their own ideas. Without much to help them they learned to cultivate the soil, even when it was rocky and poor, and to make a living from fishing in the sea and sailing their trading boats on it. Most of all, they learned to make things, at first by hand, then with machinery. Their independent thinking and living helped them to invent new things. Their industrious natures helped them manufacture successfully the new things they invented. Eli Whitney of Massachusetts invented the cotton gin and manufactured it in New Haven, Connecticut; Alexander Graham Bell invented the telephone; and many other inventions, from firearms to sewing machines, were perfected and put into use by New Englanders.

Machinery became more and more important, and hand-operated industries such as weaving, spinning, and shoemaking became machine-operated; small shops changed into big factories. The people changed, too. From experts with spinning wheel and hand loom and cobbler's tools, they changed to expert operators of big machines, to mechanics who could keep the machines running, and to supervisors and office workers who could manage big plants.

Increased production brought new people into New England, all over the region. Workers poured in from England, Ireland, Scotland,

Germany, Poland, Austria, Russia, and other countries. Many of these were skilled in the ways of making things; others were young people who learned quickly, and found great opportunity in the new land.

Growing factories mean growth in other areas, too. Railroads appeared, and the Irish came to help build them. With more people, there were better markets for farm crops, and the Portuguese, Italians, and Scandinavians came for truck farming in the lowlands and spread to other parts of the region. Portuguese and Scandinavians came, too, for the fishing and lumbering and shipbuilding. These sea-goers built a solid tradition of seafaring in New England that still is evident in every little inlet that harbors fishing and sailing boats, and in the many big ports where ocean-going ships are built, and where many can be seen, loading and unloading their interesting cargoes.

Only about one-tenth of the people in New England today are foreign-born, although many more have foreign-born parents. A large proportion of the foreign-born come from Canada; there are many French Canadian and English Canadian communities in Vermont and New Hampshire and Maine, and in other areas as well—for example, in Woonsocket, Rhode Island.

New England, then, was part of the earliest "melting pot" for which America is famous—the land of opportunity that took people from all countries and forged them into Americans. And whether they are fishermen from Portuguese ancestors, or Vermont farmers whose fore-fathers came from England, or factory workers with German or Austrian ancestry, they are now Americans, proud of New England.

47

New England Arts

Since Colonial days, New England has been a leader in America in both the excellence of her arts and crafts and in their great variety.

Many of our most beloved and most distinguished literary figures came from the New England states. Among these are Henry Wadsworth Longfellow, who wrote about New England in *The Wreck of the Hesperus, The Midnight Ride of Paul Revere, Tales of a Wayside Inn,* and many others; Louisa M. Alcott, who wrote *Little Women* and a whole series of other books about a Massachusetts family and their friends; Nathaniel Hawthorne, whose *Great Stone Face* about the face on Cannon Mountain in New Hampshire and *House of Seven Gables* are only two of his many New England stories; Laura E. Richards, whose *Captain January* is among the most famous of books for children; and Kate Douglas Wiggin, who wrote *Rebecca of Sunnybrook Farm.*

There are many others who lived and wrote in New England for many years—perhaps most or all of their lives. They include Ralph Waldo Emerson; Henry David Thoreau, whose Walden Pond is in Massachusetts; Samuel L. Clemens (Mark Twain), who wrote *Connecticut Yankee in King Arthur's Court* when he lived in Connecticut; Herman Melville, who wrote *Moby Dick* at Pittsfield, Massachusetts; and John Greenleaf Whittier and today's Robert Frost, whose poems about New England are known everywhere. Noah Webster of Connecticut authored the first dictionary of our language, published in 1828.

Famous painters and sculptors are almost as numerous. Especially well-known are the portraits of John Singleton Copley and Gilbert Stuart, and statues by Daniel Chester French and Augustus Saint-Gaudens. Examples of their work are in many museums and other public buildings of New England—in fact, all over America—along with sea paintings by Winslow Homer and Rockwell Kent, and New England landscapes by many artists. So beautiful is New England that many artists go there to spend years working, painting the sea and the many different kinds of landscapes.

Edward A. MacDowell was a distinguished composer of classical music who lived in Peterborough, New Hampshire. His home there is now the center for a colony of the arts, one of the best known of many such colonies all over New England—colonies of people engaged in music, painting, sculpture, literary arts, and handicrafts. Dramatic arts are encouraged in the same way by summer theaters in all the states; the "Players of Providence" in Rhode Island is one of the best-known of these groups.

The made-by-hand things that come from New England are many and varied. Sandwich glass was made at Sandwich, on Cape Cod, to take its place in the priceless craft products of America, even though the formula for making it was finally lost; one of the many fine collections of this rare and beautiful glassware in New England is in the Sandwich Historical Society Museum. Bennington, Vermont, potters are nationally famous for their rare Parian porcelain. Fine carvings come from nearly every state where ship figureheads and other decorations were carved during the early shipping days. Beautiful hooked rugs, quilts, and needlework of many kinds were made by the women of New England, and are still made by them. Fine silver and copperware came from the hands of such craftsmen as Paul Revere.

New England architecture is rich in buildings dating from Colonial times, with many homes, churches, and public buildings that were built when the colonies were growing. Famous among New England architects was Charles Bulfinch, who designed many beautiful homes in Boston as well as the Massachusetts State House; he was architect for the nation's Capitol in Washington, D. C., during the years 1817 to 1830.

Education and Research

From earliest Colonial days, education has been an important part of the life of New England; Massachusetts, especially, took the lead. Her famous "Dame Schools," in which a woman of a neighborhood taught the young children, were the beginning; the minister often taught the boys of the community. Gradually these schools, held in other New England colonies as well, gave way to town schools, as each town of fifty or more families came to establish a public school for its children.

Horace Mann, recognized as the "father" of the American public schools system, came from Massachusetts and helped to establish there the first state board of education in the United States. He founded one of the first schools for training teachers; other New England states, especially Vermont, early established teachers' schools as well as universities supported by the state.

Some of the leading educational institutions of our day were started in the early years of New England. Two of the best known are Harvard

University at Cambridge, Massachusetts, founded in 1636, and Yale University at New Haven, Connecticut, dating from 1701. Smith College at Northampton and Wellesley College at Wellesley, both in Massachusetts, are well-known colleges for women.

Massachusetts Institute of Technology at Cambridge is one of the country's finest schools for science and applied science, and is a leader in the tremendous research in technology carried on in New England. This is a field where the government and industrial leaders co-operate to maintain the finest of laboratories. From these laboratories come many of the improved materials and methods in use today all over the world.

Medical research, too, has an important position in New England, with Boston a leader. From Boston hospitals have come many of the discoveries in medicine made in recent years. People from all over the world come to Boston clinics for diagnosis and treatment, feeling that here they will find some of the most expert and up-to-the-minute medical knowledge to be had.

Things to think about

Why is New England the largest manufacturing region in the United States?

How do various natural resources help this region to prosper? What are these resources and how are they used?

Why is wide-spread farming less important in New England than in other sections of the country?

What things attracted people from many different countries to New England?

Why has New England long been noted for the excellence and variety of her arts and crafts?

In what ways have the Northeastern States been leaders in education?

New England enchantment and charm

Many kinds of land and water make up the enchantment of New England. There are huge bays and sounds and little inlets, and, of course, the ocean itself. There are big lakes and broad, quiet rivers —and rushing rivers as well, with waterfalls and thousands of high mountain lakes. There are rugged mountains and rolling hills and green-pastured valleys and farms and quaint villages.

There are hundreds of historical sites and relics that go back to the day when the Pilgrims landed at Plymouth, and that tell the story of how our country grew. Everywhere in New England, enchantment is just around the corner.

Water Fun

From the southwest boundary of Connecticut to the mouth of the St. Croix River on Maine's northeast coast, the ocean offers fun. Starting with Stamford and Norwalk in Connecticut, almost every town on the coast has its fine beaches, its boat clubs, and places where visitors can moor their boats in inlet, sound, or bay. At some places there seem to be more people in boats on the water than in cars on the land. Fishing, too, goes on all along the coast, with fishing boats and tackle for hire at every little town.

Cape Cod is a famous center for all this, along with the islands south of it, Martha's Vineyard and Nantucket. From Woods Hole, where there is a noted United States Fish and Wildlife Service aquarium, ferries run to these islands. There are all sorts of things to do on the islands—swimming, sun-bathing, boating, hiking, bicycling, sight-seeing, and digging for treasure. You can visit an Indian village and see an old, old lighthouse at Gay Head, on Martha's Vineyard, and you can see a lobster hatchery, where young lobsters are raised to restock the great beds of the Massachusetts coast.

Through New Hampshire and southern Maine, the fine beaches continue. In northern Maine they give way to rocky headlands, although there are still good beaches scattered between them. But here the shoreline is broken by deep inlets and islands and peninsulas where the sea rolls over wide stretches of rocks and pounds all day against rocky cliffs that edge the land.

Acadia National Park

One of the best places to enjoy the coast of Maine is in Acadia National Park, on Mount Desert Island off the northern coast. There you are surrounded by the sea pounding away at the rocky shores. Cadillac Mountain, in the middle of the park, is the highest point on the Atlantic Coast. You can drive to the summit for a view of the whole park and of miles and miles of coast and ocean and bay.

Much of the park is forested, and there are fine hikes through the woods and along the edges of lakes, where you will see deer, bear, and other wildlife. You can ride through another part of the park in an old-fashioned surrey over roads where automobiles never go. You can explore the rocky shore to see the many kinds of tidewater animals living at the edge of the sea. You can go by boat to nearby islands.

Inland Waters

Maine is a state filled with lakes and rivers. Much of the northern part of the state is still primitive wilderness. Canoes are a major means of transportation, going from lake to lake by rivers or channels that connect them. Farther south are great resort areas, around such lakes as Moosehead and Rangely, where people go for fishing, hunting, boating, and canoe trips into the wilderness.

While the other states of New England do not have as many lakes as Maine, they have some big ones, and many small ones, too. Two famous big lakes are Lake Champlain along the northwestern boundary of Vermont, and Lake Winnipesaukee in New Hampshire. In Massachusetts, Quabbin Reservoir is a big man-made lake, and so is Candlewood Lake in Connecticut. All of these lakes are great centers for resorts.

Most of the big rivers of New England empty into the Atlantic Ocean after traveling all the way east and south across the region. They come rapidly down from the highlands, and almost every river and stream has beautiful waterfalls somewhere along it. The Maine rivers, such as the Penobscot, are famous among fishermen for their great runs of ocean-going salmon. Other rivers all through New England offer fine fishing as well as beautiful scenery, from the mountain canyons in the north to the broad and lovely valley of the Connecticut River.

Scenery and Snow Fun

The White Mountains of northern New Hampshire and the Green Mountains running through most of Vermont have for many years been favorite vacation areas for people from all over the world. Superbly scenic in the summer, the White Mountains have the famous "notches" —big gaps in the mountains, through which roads and perhaps a railroad can run. Here are Franconia Notch, with its famous "Great Stone Face" of Hawthorne's story, Crawford Notch, Dixville Notch, and others. Here and all through the Green Mountains, too, highways reach high viewing places where visitors can drive and enjoy the scenery of the forested mountains and beautiful streams and lakes. Some of the high mountains, like Mount Washington in New Hampshire, have not only automobile roads to their summits, but cog-railroad and chair-lifts that take sight-seers to the top.

Similarly, the Berkshire Hills of Massachusetts and the Taconic Hills and other highlands of Connecticut offer fine scenery. All through the mountains of New England are thousands of miles of hiking trails, including the first section of the Appalachian Trail. It starts at Mount Katahdin in Maine and travels the crest of the Appalachians across Maine, New Hampshire, and Vermont.

Much of the country is included in national and state forest lands. The White Mountain National Forest alone, in New Hampshire and Maine, covers nearly a million acres. In it, as in the other forest lands, are campgrounds, fine fishing and hiking, and other fun for visitors.

There are also many fine state parks in the hills and mountains, where visitors can camp, picnic, fish, and hike in deeply wooded surroundings. Parks and forests are popular around the year. Fall brings beautiful yellows and flaming reds to the woods and people travel hundreds of miles to see this display of color.

Winter brings skiing, tobogganing, ice boating, and other winter sports. There are fine ski runs, with lifts to take skiers to the top of them, all over New England. Many of them have schools to teach beginners, and easy runs for learning to ski. Special snow trains and buses take people to the ski areas, and gay winter festivals are held at some of them. Cranmore Mountain is a famous ski area in New Hampshire, with a unique "Skimobile" that takes people to the summit; it also operates in summer for sight-seers. Mount Washington in New Hampshire, Mount Mansfield, Bread Loaf Mountain and Woodstock, in Vermont, and Sugarloaf Mountain in Maine are among many, many other winter sports centers.

Places to Go and Things to See

Famous places in history are so thick in New England that you could never see them all in one visit, or even describe all of them in one book. Many are not only famous from yesterday's events, but are still making history today. Perhaps their greatest center is Boston, landing-place of some of our country's earliest colonists and a leader in the life of this country since its history began.

Most famous of Boston's historic places is the Old North Church, where Paul Revere's friend hung a lantern to flash the news that the British were marching from Boston. Paul Revere's home still stands in Boston, restored and furnished as it was when he lived in it; it is the oldest home in Boston. The Boston Common dates from 1634 and is the oldest public park in America; it has an adjoining garden with a small lake, on which you can ride in a "swan boat." Other famous and interesting old places are Faneuil Hall where many important Colonial meetings took place, the Old State House, the Old South Meeting House, and the present State House and other buildings on Beacon Hill. A more modern center of interest in Boston is Science Park, where the Boston Museum of Science has a planetarium and other demonstrations and exhibits of natural science.

At Cambridge, just west of Boston, you can see Longfellow's home, and the famous buildings and museums of Harvard University and Massachusetts Institute of Technology. The Harvard museums include one for children at Longfellow school, a collection of beautiful flowers made of glass, and a museum of astronomy at the Harvard Observatory.

Farther west are Lexington and Concord, where the first shots of the Revolutionary War were fired. The battlegrounds are preserved today for you to see, marked by statues of the Minute Men and relics of the battles. You can see, too, the Hancock-Clarke House where Samuel Adams and John Hancock had taken refuge; Paul Revere rode there to warn them that the British were marching, and so they were able to escape.

Concord has many fine old homes of famous people, among them the Old Manse where Ralph Waldo Emerson lived, and later, Nathaniel Hawthorne; Orchard House, where Louisa May Alcott wrote *Little Women;* and Emerson House, where Emerson lived the latter part of his life. Thoreau's Walden Pond is near Concord, in Walden State Reservation.

Near Framingham is the famous old Wayside Inn, setting for Longfellow's *Tales of a Wayside Inn.* You can stay overnight and eat at the inn, and on the grounds you can see the schoolhouse of "Mary Had a Little Lamb."

Across the Charles River from Boston are Bunker and Breed's hills, where the Battle of Bunker Hill was fought; a tall monument on Breed's Hill has a stairway to the top. East of here, at the junction of the Mystic and Charles Rivers, is a 150-year-old United States Navy Yard. The famous old ship *Constitution*—nicknamed "Old Ironsides" —is docked here, and is open to visitors.

In Salem, north of Boston, you can see wharves dating from the great days of the sailing ships, and you can see some of the handsome old homes of the sea captains and the treasures they brought home on their ships. Another interesting home is the House of Seven Gables, used by Hawthorne in his story of that name. And close to the seashore an early Puritan village has been reconstructed to show the life of the Puritans who settled there.

Gloucester, still farther north, is gateway to Cape Ann and Gloucester Harbor, which has long been a favorite harbor for hundreds of fishing boats. There is a fine lighthouse on Cape Ann—one of many along the shore—and there are dozens of beautiful old buildings in the town.

At Plymouth, south of Boston, the first things a sight-seer wants to see are historic Plymouth Rock, and, in the harbor, a replica of the *Mayflower.* Plymouth Village has been reconstructed. In one of the oldest houses you can see pottery made and household handicrafts performed by workers in costume. In the towns of Cape Cod, too, are many old homes, Cape Cod cottages, and old churches. Provincetown has the Pilgrim Monument, marking the first landing of the Pilgrims.

Falmouth, on the southern tip of the Cape, was once a whaling and shipbuilding center. Martha's Vineyard and Nantucket Island have fine harbors and were once the home port for whaling vessels. Today in their museums are many fine collections and exhibits from the old whaling days.

In western Massachusetts, too, there are many places of great historical interest—old homes that have survived, old churches, meeting houses, and sometimes whole villages that have been restored as they were in the state's early years. Chief among these is Old Sturbridge Village, with a grist mill, tavern, crafts center, blacksmith shop, meeting house, and other shops and stores, as well as old homes of the villagers.

Just as it is in Massachusetts, history is alive in the other states of New England. Each of them has many towns and villages with buildings and village green that date from Colonial days. Guilford, Connecticut, is one of these, with fine old homes, churches, and other buildings; others are Windsor and Granby, where tobacco has been grown since 1640. Woodstock, Vermont is another interesting "Colonial" village, and Old Bennington has buildings from Revolutionary War days and relics from the important battle fought near by. Almost every old town or city that you visit in New England will have homes and churches of historic interest.

Many of the old homes are preserved as the birthplace or home of some famous person. In New Hampshire the birthplace of Daniel Webster, a two-room cabin near Franklin, is now a museum. At Cornish is the studio of the sculptor, Saint-Gaudens, preserved as a memorial to him.

In western Vermont, the country where Ethan Allen led his Green Mountain Boys against the English, there are statues of Allen and his followers in some of the towns; Allen's home is at Arlington. In Connecticut a school teacher named Nathan Hale left his teaching to become a special agent for the Continental Army in the Revolution, and lost his life when he was caught, regretting that "I have only one life to lose for my country." His home is preserved at Manchester, and Connecticut Hall, where he lived when he attended Yale, is among the historic buildings of Yale University at New Haven.

Bridgeport was the home of Tom Thumb, the famous midget in the Barnum and Bailey circus. One of the owners, P. T. Barnum, lived in Bridgeport. In Rhode Island a park and statues and other monuments in Providence remind you that Roger Williams founded Providence in 1636 in Indian wilderness. Portland, Maine, has the Wadsworth Longfellow House, where the poet was born and lived for many years; it is a museum furnished with many of his belongings. In the city is a square named "Longfellow," with a famous statue of him.

Coastal cities are likely to have shipyards that grew when sailing vessels were being built. Maine had bustling yards at Kennebunk, Kennebunkport, Kittery, Bath, and other ports. The Portsmouth Navy Yard is still at Kittery and across the river at Portsmouth, New Hampshire. Here the *Ranger* was built, flagship of John Paul Jones in the early days of the American Navy. New London and Groton, Connecticut, are old whaling ports and have whaling museums. Today they are home to the United States Coast Guard Academy and the North Atlantic submarine fleet. Mystic is another old shipbuilding center, and still has interesting boat yards.

Much of the history of New England is bound up with its manufacturing, and as you visit some of the factories today, you learn that parts of the plants have come down from the early years. In Manchester, New Hampshire, are some of the oldest textile mills, and there are various museums in the city exhibiting other manufactured products, from handicrafts to locomotives and fire engines. Similarly, in any city where manufacturing has been going on through the years, you will find interesting exhibits of its history.

Fine museums are a hallmark of New England: among the most famous is the Marine Museum at Mystic, Connecticut, a feature of the restored Village of Mystic Seaport. The museum preserves all kinds of boats and seafaring gear, including the last old whaling ship, the *Charles W. Morgan*. In the museum in the State Capitol at Montpelier, Vermont, is the Stephen Day Press, first printing press to be used in the American colonies.

Old lighthouses have been preserved all along the New England coast. One of the best of these is on Block Island, off the Rhode Island mainland. Here, too, is a tradition of treasure buried by Captain Kidd, the object of much futile digging by visitors. But when they dig for history's treasures anywhere in New England, they find them in great measure.

Things to think about

Why are many areas in New England year-round resorts for both natives and visitors?

How do lakes, rivers, and the ocean provide enchantment?

How do the mountains contribute to the enchantment of New England?

Why is much of New England's enchantment closely tied to history?

Why is the tourist industry one of New England's leading industries?

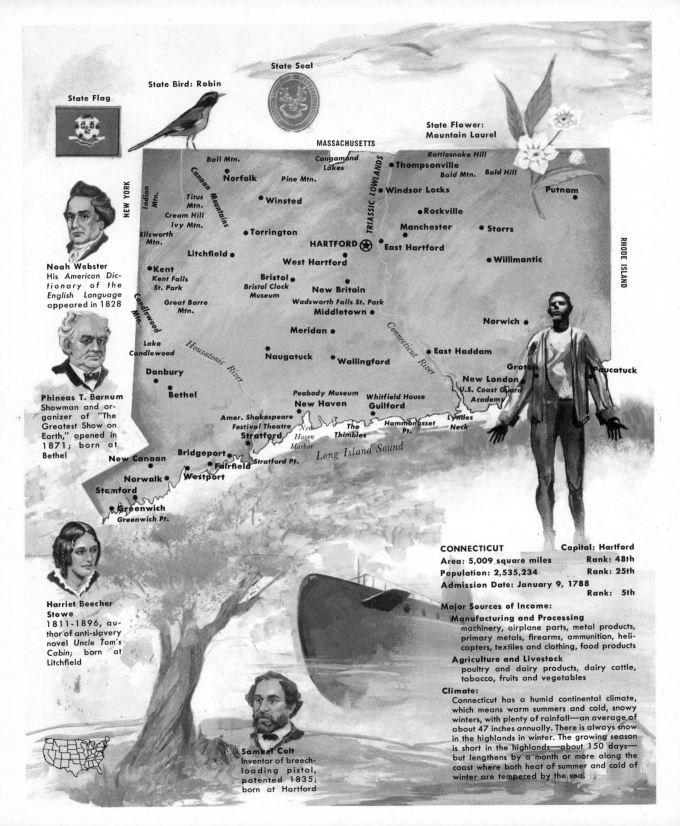

State Flag

State Bird: Robin

State Seal

State Flower: Mountain Laurel

MASSACHUSETTS

NEW YORK

RHODE ISLAND

Noah Webster
His *American Dictionary of the English Language* appeared in 1828

Phineas T. Barnum
Showman and organizer of "The Greatest Show on Earth," opened in 1871; born at Bethel

Harriet Beecher Stowe
1811-1896, author of anti-slavery novel *Uncle Tom's Cabin*; born at Litchfield

Samuel Colt
Inventor of breech-loading pistol, patented 1835; born at Hartford

Ball Mtn.
Congamond Lakes
Rattlesnake Hill
Pine Mtn.
Bald Mtn.
Bald Hill
Norfolk
Thompsonville
Putnam
Indian Mtn.
Titus Mtn.
Winsted
Windsor Locks
Cream Hill
Ivy Mtn.
Rockville
Ellsworth Mtn.
Torrington
Manchester
Storrs
HARTFORD
East Hartford
Litchfield
West Hartford
Willimantic
Kent
Kent Falls St. Park
Bristol
Bristol Clock Museum
New Britain
Great Barre Mtn.
Wadsworth Falls St. Park
Middletown
Norwich
Meridan
Lake Candlewood
Naugatuck
Wallingford
East Haddam
Danbury
Groton
New London
U.S. Coast Guard Academy
Pacuatuck
Bethel
Peabody Museum
New Haven
Whitfield House
Guilford
Amer. Shakespeare Festival Theatre
Stratford
New Haven Harbor
The Thimbles
Hammonasset Pt.
Lyndes Neck
Bridgeport
Fairfield
Stratford Pt.
Long Island Sound
New Canaan
Norwalk
Westport
Stamford
Greenwich
Greenwich Pt.

Canaan Mountains
Candlewood Mtn.
Housatonic River
Connecticut River
TRIASSIC LOWLANDS

CONNECTICUT

Area: 5,009 square miles

Population: 2,535,234

Admission Date: January 9, 1788

Capital: Hartford

Rank: 48th

Rank: 25th

Rank: 5th

Major Sources of Income:

Manufacturing and Processing
machinery, airplane parts, metal products, primary metals, firearms, ammunition, helicopters, textiles and clothing, food products

Agriculture and Livestock
poultry and dairy products, dairy cattle, tobacco, fruits and vegetables

Climate:
Connecticut has a humid continental climate, which means warm summers and cold, snowy winters, with plenty of rainfall—an average of about 47 inches annually. There is always snow in the highlands in winter. The growing season is short in the highlands—about 150 days— but lengthens by a month or more along the coast where both heat of summer and cold of winter are tempered by the sea.

In New England, only Rhode Island is smaller than Connecticut; in the United States outside of New England, only Delaware is smaller. Yet Connecticut early took an important place in the life of the United States, and continues to hold it.

Connecticut was founded by people who wanted independence in politics and religion. One of the thirteen original states, she was first to declare her independence from England. Her people were hard-working, and they were also imaginative and ingenious when it came to finding new ways of doing their work. In no other state were there so many inventions as in Connecticut. Machines, from sewing machines to submarines, came from there, and processes such as condensing milk and vulcanizing rubber. Yale locks and Colt revolvers, ball bearings and pins and needles, helicopters and airplane propellers, are other products that this state gives us. There are hundreds of others, many of them requiring great skill and precision to make them successfully.

Important Whens and Whats in the Making of Connecticut

1614 Adriaen Block, a Dutch navigator, discovers and explores the Connecticut River.

1633 The Dutch set up a trading post at what is now Hartford.

1633-1638 English colonists from Massachusetts build Wethersfield, Windsor, and New Haven.

1639 The towns unite in a commonwealth and draw up a constitution to govern them.

1654 The English take over all Dutch claims.

1662 The colony receives a royal charter from King Charles II of England.

1687 The royal charter is recalled but patriots hide it from the English governor in the "Charter Oak" at Hartford.

1788 Connecticut becomes the fifth state in the Union after ratifying the United States Constitution.

Back in the days when all this was beginning, "Yankee Peddlers" carried the first manufactured products, such as tin utensils, in packs on their backs or in horse-drawn wagons, to the pioneer homes. Returning, they brought word of other goods that were needed, and so manufacturing grew up to meet the need.

This was the beginning of the great manufacturing industries of the state. Then, as now, the name "Connecticut Yankees" was used for the people of the state, and meant people who work with great industry and skill to manufacture goods of many different kinds. It is likely that you never go through a day without using something manufactured in Connecticut—your rubbers or your bicycle, the carpet on your floor, your hand-ax, the lock on your door, the knife and fork you eat with, probably came from Hartford or New Haven or Waterbury or some other manufacturing center in Connecticut.

Hartford is a center of another kind, also. Here was started the first insurance in the United States, and Hartford today, called "The Insurance City," is the world's greatest insurance center.

Connecticut has two hundred miles of shoreline along her southern boundary, and here are wonderful beaches, as well as port cities that have come down from Colonial times, through the thrilling days of the whalers and the clippers. Here, too, especially toward the west, are towns and suburbs where people live who work in New York City, and ride back and forth from their homes to their work.

Connecticut has the broad Connecticut Valley and other river valleys, where farms produce poultry and hay and dairy cattle—and tobacco. Some of the tobacco is "shade-grown"—grown under tents of porous cloth that cover many acres—and is the most expensive tobacco grown anywhere.

There are more than a thousand small lakes in Connecticut, besides man-made Lake Candlewood in the southwest corner. These and the many fine state parks and state forests are popular areas for recreation, summer and winter.

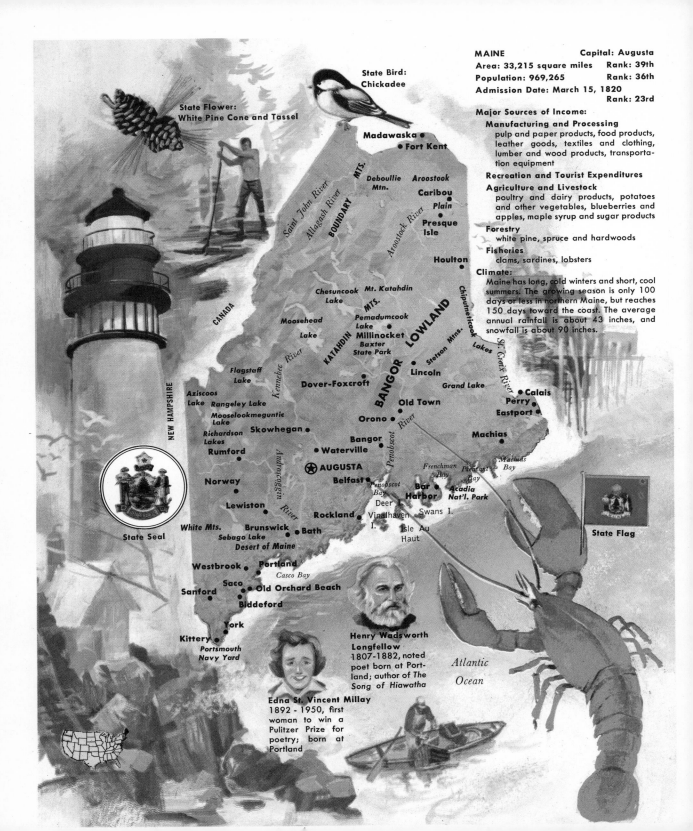

State Flower:
White Pine Cone and Tassel

State Bird:
Chickadee

MAINE **Capital: Augusta**
Area: 33,215 square miles **Rank: 39th**
Population: 969,265 **Rank: 36th**
Admission Date: March 15, 1820
Rank: 23rd

Major Sources of Income:

Manufacturing and Processing
pulp and paper products, food products, leather goods, textiles and clothing, lumber and wood products, transportation equipment

Recreation and Tourist Expenditures

Agriculture and Livestock
poultry and dairy products, potatoes and other vegetables, blueberries and apples, maple syrup and sugar products

Forestry
white pine, spruce and hardwoods

Fisheries
clams, sardines, lobsters

Climate:
Maine has long, cold winters and short, cool summers. The growing season is only 100 days or less in northern Maine, but reaches 150 days toward the coast. The average annual rainfall is about 43 inches, and snowfall is about 90 inches.

Madawaska
Fort Kent

Saint John River
Allagash River
Aroostook River

Deboullie Mtn.
Aroostook
Caribou
Plain
Presque Isle

BOUNDARY MTS.

Houlton

CANADA

Chesuncook Lake
Mt. Katahdin
MTS.
Pemadumcook Lake
Millinocket
Baxter State Park

Moosehead Lake

KATAHDIN

Chiputneticook Lakes
St. Croix River

Flagstaff Lake

Kennebec River

Dover-Foxcroft

BANGOR LOWLAND

Stetson Mtns.

Lincoln
Grand Lake

Calais
Perry
Eastport

Old Town

NEW HAMPSHIRE

Aziscoos Lake
Rangeley Lake
Mooselookmeguntic Lake
Richardson Lakes

Skowhegan

Orono

Penobscot River

Machias

Rumford

Androscoggin River

Bangor
Waterville

★ AUGUSTA
Belfast

Machias Bay

Frenchman Bay
Pleasant Bay

Norway

Penobscot Bay
Deer I.
Vinalhaven I.

Bar Harbor
Acadia Nat'l. Park
Swans I.
Isle Au Haut

Lewiston

Rockland

State Seal

White Mts.
Brunswick
Bath
Sebago Lake
Desert of Maine

Westbrook
Portland
Casco Bay

Sanford
Saco
Old Orchard Beach
Biddeford

York

Kittery
Portsmouth Navy Yard

State Flag

Henry Wadsworth Longfellow
1807-1882, noted poet born at Portland; author of The Song of Hiawatha

Edna St. Vincent Millay
1892 - 1950, first woman to win a Pulitzer Prize for poetry; born at Portland

Atlantic Ocean

Maine is by far the largest state in New England; and it would seem that this largest state is almost as much water as it is land. The whole long southeastern edge, bordered by the Atlantic Ocean, is deeply indented by big bays and inlets, forming hundreds of peninsulas and islands washed by the sea. One great river after another empties into the sea, their mouths drowned for many miles inland by ocean water. Hundreds of rivers flow through the state, most of them south to the ocean; but some flow north to Canada's St. John River. And scattered far and wide over Maine are hundreds on hundreds of lakes, ranging in size from ponds in a city park to forty-mile-long Moosehead Lake in the central part of the state.

Important Whens and Whats in the Making of Maine

1497 English explorer John Cabot sails the Maine coast.

1604 French explorer Samuel de Champlain, founds a colony on St. Croix Island.

1608 The first ship in America, the *Virginia,* is built at Popham.

1630 The first permanent colony is settled by the English at Saco.

1642 Georgeana, New York, becomes the first incorporated town in the colonies.

1691 The royal charter granted to the Massachusetts colony includes Maine as part of that colony.

1775 Falmouth, now Portland, is shelled and virtually destroyed by the British fleet at the outbreak of the Revolutionary War.

1777 John Paul Jones' *Ranger,* the first ship to fly the American flag, is built and launched at Kittery.

1788 Maine enters the Union as part of Massachusetts.

1820 Maine, separated from Massachusetts, enters the Union as the 23rd state.

1842 Maine's northern boundary is established by a treaty with Canada.

How do people use all this water? They use the water of the sea for fishing, for fun and for a living. Great quantities of herring are packed as sardines. Lobsters are shipped all over the world. For boating, fishing, hunting, and camping, people use the lakes in Maine's wonderful forests; toward the north, these still cover thousands of acres of wilderness. More than two-thirds of Maine is forested, in white pine, balsam, fir, hemlock, and spruce, and oak, birch, maple, and others. Bear, deer, and many small animals are sheltered by the forests, and there are moose in the central and northern lake and swamp region.

The big rivers with their deep, drowned channels, are used for transportation, and manufacturing cities have grown up on them. Bangor and Augusta and Lewiston are cities that use a river's power to manufacture paper and paper pulp, textiles, wood products and lumber, and the river's water to ship them to market. Portland manufactures these and many other products, and processes fish and other foods, as well as serving as the state's largest ocean port and shipping center.

Poultry-raising and general farming and dairying take place in much of the southern half of Maine. In the northeast corner, in Aroostook County, such quantities of potatoes are grown that the state is one of America's greatest producers. And Maine is by far the greatest producer of blueberries.

The mountains of Maine are part of the Appalachians, and have their highest point in the state on Mount Katahdin. Here is the beginning of the Appalachian Trail, famous footpath that follows the crest of the Appalachians all the way south into Georgia.

State Flag

**State Flower:
Mayflower**

**State Bird:
Chickadee**

**Alexander Graham
Bell**
Invented the first
successful tele-
phone in 1875

John Quincy Adams
Sixth President
of the U.S., 1825-
1829; son of John
Adams

John Adams
Second President
of the U.S., 1797-
1801

VERMONT

NEW HAMPSHIRE

Newburyport

NEW YORK

Mt. Greylock
Adams

Athol

Lawrence

*Halibut Pt.
Fishermen's Mem.*

Gardner

Lowell

Andover

Greenfield

Fitchburg

House of Salem
Seven Gables

Gloucester

Leominster
Concord

*Massachusetts
Bay*

Lexington

Lynn

Quabbin
Reservoir

Walden Pond

Cambridge

Amherst

BOSTON

Boston Bay

Marlboro

Northampton

Worcester

Brookline

Bunker Hill Mon.

South Hadley

Wellesley

Quincy

Holyoke

*Old Sturbridge
Village*

Blue Hills

Chicopee

Cape Cod

Springfield

Southbridge

Webster

Brockton

Provincetown
Pilgrim Mon.

CONNECTICUT

Plymouth Bay

RHODE ISLAND

Attleboro

*Narragansett
Basin*

Plymouth
Plymouth Rock

Cape Cod Bay

Fall River

Cape Cod
Canal

Sandwich

CAPE COD

New
Bedford

Monomoy I.

Woods Hole

Nantucket Sound

Buzzards Bay

Elizabeth Islands

*Vineyard
Sound*

Martha's Vineyard

Nantucket I.

Atlantic Ocean

TACONIC Range

HOOSAC Range

BERKSHIRE HILLS

Connecticut River

LOWLANDS

TRIASSIC

Pittsfield

Lenox

*Mt.
Everett*

State Seal

MASSACHUSETTS

Area: 8,257 square miles   Capital: Boston

Population: 5,148,578   Rank: 45th

Admission Date: February 6, 1788   Rank: 9th

                                 Rank: 6th

Major Sources of Income:

Manufacturing and Processing
electrical and other machinery and equipment, textiles and clothing, food products, printing and pub-
lishing, leather and leather goods, metal products,
pulp and paper products

Agriculture and Livestock
poultry and dairy products, truck crops, beef cattle,
fruits, potatoes and cranberries

Fisheries

Recreation and Tourist Expenditures

Climate:
Massachusetts, in general, has a humid continental
climate—cold winters and hot, humid summers. There
is an annual rainfall of about 40 inches and a growing
season of 150 days; along the coast the growing
season reaches about 190 days. The coastal area is
cooler in summer and warmer in winter. Hurricanes
blowing up from the south sometimes do great dam-
age along the coast, and the famous "nor-easter"
windstorms, blowing from the northeast, are part of
the coast's winter weather.

Massachusetts is a long rectangle that reaches all the way from the Atlantic Ocean to the boundary of New York. It is a fine cross section of all the kinds of country we find in New England.

Almost the whole eastern quarter is Coastal Plain, including the huge hook of Cape Cod and the islands of Martha's Vineyard and Nantucket. All of the area is so low that there is much marshland, like the vast cranberry bogs of Cape Cod. The whole coastline is a series of slender peninsulas stabbing into the sea, often with near-by islands. Back from the coast is a rolling country of green meadows, truck farms, and ponds and small lakes.

Important Whens and Whats in the Making of Massachusetts

1497-1498	English explorer John Cabot sails along the coast.
1602	Bartholomew Gosnold lands near what is now New Bedford, discovers and names Cape Cod.
1614	Captain John Smith makes the first map of Massachusetts land.
1620	The Pilgrims in the *Mayflower* land at Plymouth.
1621	The first Thanksgiving is observed.
1630	The Massachusetts Bay Colony and Boston are established.
1675-1676	King Philip's War brings an end to fur trade and all but erases Indian tribal life in the southern New England region.
1773	The Boston Tea Party occurs when a group of irate colonists, disguised as Indians, throw English tea into Boston Harbor.
1775	The first battles in the War of Independence are fought at Lexington and Concord.
1788	Massachusetts, including Maine, ratifies the United States Constitution and becomes the sixth state in the Union.
1819	Maine is separated from Massachusetts.

Then the land lifts to a low plateau about 1,000 feet above sea level. This highland area of low, rolling hills continues west to the broad and fertile Connecticut River Valley, often called the Pioneer Valley in Massachusetts. West of the valley are the beautiful Berkshire Hills, a continuation of the Green Mountains to the north.

Boston, biggest city in New England, is on Massachusetts' coast, built on her finest natural harbor at the mouths of the Charles and Mystic Rivers. The city was originally built on a peninsula jutting into the bay, and in Revolutionary times was connected to the mainland by only a narrow neck of land. Today much of the bay has been filled in, and so now the peninsula that holds Boston is broad and substantial. Other cities have built up so close to Boston that all around is a big metropolitan area where one city runs into another. From here come many of the manufactured products of New England; and Boston's waterfront has one of the biggest fishery centers in America. Her harbor is a busy one and at Logan International Airport, lying off the harbor, the biggest of jet airplanes can land and take off.

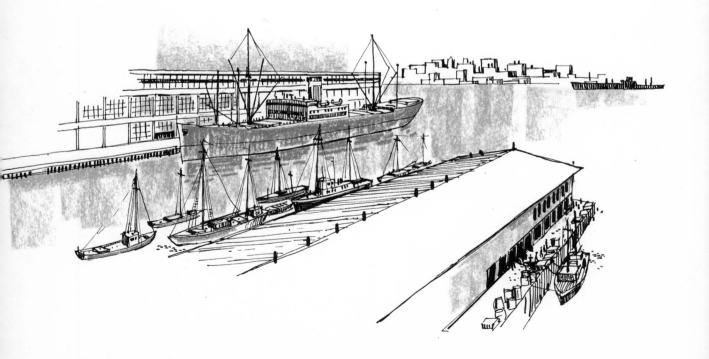

In other large cities, factories turn out all sorts of precision products, textiles, shoes and other leather goods, paper—all the products that have come for years from New England. Some of the industries date back to the days when manufacturing began in America, and some make new products such as airplane parts and electronic equipment. Coastal industrial cities include Fall River, in the south, and Lynn, north of Boston. Inland are Lowell, in the north; Worcester, west of Boston; Springfield and Holyoke, on the Connecticut River; Pittsfield, in the west; and various others. They are connected by a network of express highways that allow motorists to travel quickly to almost any part of the state.

Massachusetts has a great many state parks, reservations, and forests where her people and visitors enjoy fishing, swimming, camping, and other outdoor recreation. They range from beach parks on the coast to Greylock State Reservation in the northwest, where scenic Mount Greylock is the highest point in the Berkshires. A famous annual event in the Berkshires is the Tanglewood Festival at Lenox, where people from all over the world come to enjoy and learn more about music.

Massachusetts is sometimes called "the cradle of American liberty," because the state's early life and development formed so much of the beginning of liberty in this country, and helped to lay the groundwork of the government of the United States.

State Seal

State Bird:
Purple Finch

State Flower:
Purple Lilac

State Flag

CANADA

Halls Stream

Connecticut River

Colebrook

Whitcomb Mtn.

Pilot Range

Androscoggin River

Lancaster

Gardner Mtn.   Littleton   Crescent Range   Berlin

Lisbon   Presidential Range   Mt. Washington

The Great Stone Face   WHITE   MOUNTAINS
Franconia Notch

Crawford Notch
Glenn Ellis Falls

Cranmore Mtn.

North Woodstock
Sugar Hill

Saco River

VERMONT

Moose Mtn.   Polar Caves   Sandwich Range   Conway

Plymouth   Squam Lake   Ossipee Mts.

Ashland   Meredith

Hanover   Bristol   Wolfeboro
Laconia   Lake Winnipesaukee

Lebanon   Belknap Mts.

Croydon Mtn.   Shaker Village

Salmon Falls River

MAINE

Newport   Rochester

Claremont
Saint-Gaudens Mem.   Sunapee Mtn.   Blue Hill Range   Dover

CONCORD ⊛   Durham

Hillsboro

Great Bay

Pulpit Rocks   Manchester   Portsmouth

Keene   MacDowell Colony   Cavern   Exeter   Atlantic Ocean
Peterborough   Amherst

Winchester   Milford
Cathedral of the Pines   Nashua

Merrimack River

Connecticut River

MASSACHUSETTS

Franklin Pierce
14th President of the U.S., 1853-1857; born at Hillsboro

Horace Greeley
1811-1872, news-paper editor and founder of the New York Tribune; born at Amherst

Daniel Webster
1782-1852, states-man, lawyer and orator; born at Franklin

NEW HAMPSHIRE

Capital: Concord

Area: 9,304 square miles
Rank: 44th

Population: 606,921   Rank: 45th

Admission Date: June 21, 1788
Rank: 9th

Major Sources of Income:

Manufacturing and Processing leather products, machinery, tex-tiles and clothing, pulp and paper products

Agriculture and Livestock poultry and dairy products, ap-ples and other fruits, potatoes, hay and garden crops, maple syrup and sugar products

Forestry

Recreation and Tourist Expenditures

Climate:
New Hampshire summers are cool and pleasant, but the winters are long and severe, with as much as 150 inches of snowfall in the moun-tains. Toward the coast, snowfall averages about 50 inches. Rainfall varies from 35 inches in the coastal area to 50 inches in the mountains.

New Hampshire and Vermont are both long, narrow wedges, New Hampshire lying with its point toward the north. Together they make a chunky oblong, through which the Connecticut River is a diagonal dividing line between the two states.

The northern half of New Hampshire holds the White Mountains, some of the most famous and scenic mountains in America. They are made up of various high and rugged ranges, such as the Presidential Range and the Franconia Mountains. Especially in these more southern ranges, many peaks rise to more than 5,000 feet. Highest point in the Northeastern States is Mount Washington in the Presidential Range, rising to 6,288 feet. In the northern part of the state, the height of the peaks drops off to about 3,000 feet. The mountains are heavily forested with spruce, white pine, hemlock, fir, maple, and oak.

Important Whens and Whats in the Making of New Hampshire

1605 French explorer Samuel de Champlain explores the coast.

1614 Captain John Smith explores the coast and the Isles of Shoals.

1623 Under an English land grant to Captain John Mason, settlements are established at Dover, Portsmouth, Exeter and Hampton.

1629 Captain Mason names the eastern lands granted to him, New Hampshire.

1639 Massachusetts claims New Hampshire as part of the Massachusetts Bay Colony.

1679 New Hampshire receives a royal charter as a separate colony from the king of England.

1754-1763 French and Indian War.

1776 New Hampshire adopts a constitution and forms a state government independent of England.

1788 After ratifying the United States Constitution, New Hampshire becomes the ninth state of the Union.

The mountains are a major reason for New Hampshire's biggest industry, the tourist business. Rising in peaks and shoulder-cliffs of solid, gleaming granite, with deep valleys and gorges between, they are superbly beautiful. Here are the "notches"—deep gaps in the mountain chains set off by steep-faced granite cliffs, with often a mountain stream and a waterfall or two. Typical of these is Franconia Notch near North Woodstock, where the cliffs form "The Great Stone Face."

The vast White Mountain National Forest, spilling over into Maine, and various state parks preserve much of the mountain area for recreation. In summer there are hiking, camping, fishing, and hunting, and in winter nearly every mountainside is the scene of skiing and other winter sports. Among many famous centers are Cannon Mountain near Franconia Notch, Mount Washington, and Cranmore Mountain near North Conway. Many of these centers have ski lifts or tramways that take sightseers to the top of the mountain in summer, and some of them have scenic highways to the crest. Winter sports often include an annual winter carnival; most famous of these is the one at Hanover, sponsored by Dartmouth College.

In the central part of New Hampshire is big Lake Winnipesaukee, almost as important an attraction for vacationers as the mountains. It offers all kinds of boat fun, including steamer excursions from one resort town to another, as well as fishing and swimming from fine beaches. Winter sports, too, are popular here.

South of the lake is the Merrimack Valley, which, with the Connecticut Valley, represents the largest agricultural lands of the state. The Merrimack River, falling fast from the highlands, furnishes the power for Manchester, New Hampshire's largest city. Here are manufactured such products as boots and shoes, textiles, machinery, electrical equipment, and wood products, including lumber and paper. The state's second largest city, Concord, is also on the Merrimack; Concord adds important granite quarries to its industries.

New Hampshire's short seacoast on the Atlantic has the historic port of Portsmouth, shipping and commercial center for the state. Portsmouth is across the Piscataqua River from Kittery, Maine, and these two have been a shipbuilding and shipping center since shipbuilding began in America. They are today an important base for the United States Navy.

State Bird:
Rhode Island Red Hen

State Seal

State Flag

State Flower:
Violet

Slatersville

Pascoag • Harrisville

Woonsocket

Woonsocket Hill

Blackstone River

RHODE ISLAND Capital: Providence
Area: 1,214 square miles Rank: 50th
Population: 859,488   Rank: 39th
Admission Date: May 29, 1790
                          Rank: 13th

Major Sources of Income:
Manufacturing and Processing
textiles, machinery, food products,
primary metals, metal products, jewelry and silverware, rubber products

Agriculture and Livestock
poultry and dairy products, potatoes and truck crops, apples

Fisheries

Recreation and Tourist Expenditures

Climate:
Rhode Island's climate is very mild compared with the climates of the other
New England states. Nearby water
makes the winters balmy and the summers cool. There is an average rainfall
of about 38 inches a year. Only about
30 inches of snow falls through the
winter.

Jerimoth Hill

Valley Falls
Central Falls
Pawtucket
Old Slater Mill

PROVIDENCE ☆

Roger Williams Park

Barden Res.

Cranston

Scituate Reservoir Kent Dam

West Warwick

Coventry • Quidnick

Warwick

Greenwich Bay

East Greenwich

Providence River

Tenmile River

MASSACHUSETTS

Barrington

Warren

Bristol

Mount Hope Bay

Prudence I.

Portsmouth

Narragansett Bay

Sakonnet River

Rhode Island Red Mon.

Adamsville

Nonquit Pond

Middletown

Conanicut

Aquidneck Island

Quicksand Pond

Wickford

Island

Hope Valley

Kingston

Great Swamp Wildlife Res.

Newport

Sakonnet

Sakonnet Pt.

Rhode Island Sound

Wakefield

Narragansett

Worden Pond

Ashaway

Bradford

Point Judith Pond

CONNECTICUT

Westerly

Quonochontaug Pond

Noyes Pt.

Ninigret Pond

Point Judith

Pawcatuck River

Napatree Pt.

Block Island Sound

Great Salt Pond

Block Island

Nathanael Greene
1742-1786, Rev-
olutionary War
general

Commodore Oliver Perry
1785-1819; Noted for
his victory over the
British in the battle of
Lake Erie during the
War of 1812

Ambrose Burnside
Union general in
the Civil War and
Governor of Rhode
Island, 1866-1869

Rhode Island is the United States' smallest state. Nevertheless, the state has more people per square mile—about 800—than any other. This is far in excess of the national average of 50 people per square mile.

The most spectacular physical feature of Rhode Island is the complex of bays and inlets that invades her southeastern corner and almost splits the state in half. Narragansett Bay is the largest of these. The bays are the drowned mouths of several rivers—the Blackstone and the Taunton and several smaller ones that empty in this area. The Sakonnet and the Providence and others are called rivers, but are actually salt bays and inlets that have invaded the land.

Important Whens and Whats in the Making of Rhode Island

1524   Giovanni da Verrazano, Italian navigator and explorer in the service of France, explores the coast and reports the land is similar to the Isle of Rhodes.

1614   Adriaen Block, Dutch navigator, lands on what is now Block Island.

1636   Roger Williams, exiled from Massachusetts Bay Colony, founds Providence.

1638   Anne Hutchinson and others establish a colony on Aquidneck Island. Other colonies follow.

1647   The several colonies combine under one government.

1663   England's King Charles II grants a charter to the colonists.

1675-1676   King Philip's War brings an end to fur trade and all but erases Indian tribal life in the southern New England area.

1776   Rhode Island declares her independence from England.

1790   Rhode Island ratifies the United States Constitution and becomes the 13th of the original thirteen states.

So much sea within its borders has made Rhode Island a seafaring state from colonial days. Whaling, shipping, and shipbuilding were major industries in the state's early history; shipping and building of ships and pleasure boats are still of major importance.

Providence was Rhode Island's first town and is today its largest city. The city lies on several rivers and uses their power to manufacture such things as jewelry and silverware, machinery, rubber goods, plastics, and electronic equipment. And Providence lies at the head of the system of bays and uses their waters to ship these products from a fine harbor. Providence is rich in the things that bring so many people to live in Rhode Island—a pleasant, ocean-side climate, wonderful recreation on open water, and means of earning a good living in one of the many manufacturing plants. Other manufacturing cities include Pawtucket, East Providence, and Cranston, near Providence; and Woonsocket, Warwick, and others. Important bay-area cities include Newport, Bristol, Warren, and Barrington.

There are many peninsulas and islands in the bay. Largest of the islands is Aquidneck, also called Rhode Island; others are Conanicut and Prudence. They have fine beaches and small harbors for pleasure boats, and are given over largely to resorts and homes. Newport, at the southern end of Aquidneck Island, is one of the most famous fashionable resorts in the world. Bridges from the mainland reach Aquidneck and Conanicut; ferries run to them and various other islands.

Lobster, mackerel, herring, and bluefish are taken from the waters of the bay and the sounds off Rhode Island's shores. Block Island, ten miles offshore in Block Island Sound, bases fleets that fish for tuna and swordfish.

From the sandy lowlands around the bays, the land rises quickly toward the north and west to become sharply hilly, with many lakes and valleys between the hills. Biggest lake is Scituate Reservoir in the center of the state. Less than half the area of the state is forested, and there are many dairy and poultry farms and truck gardens.

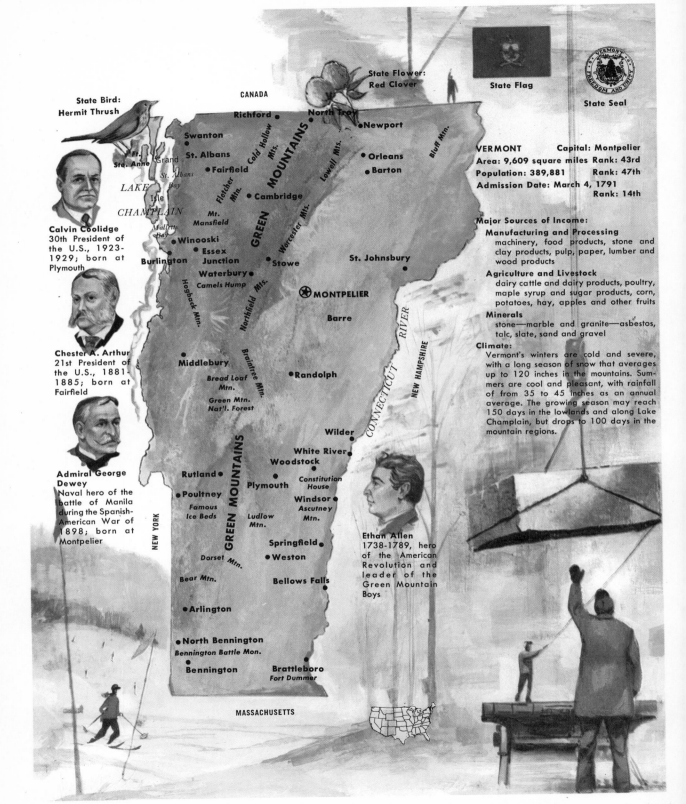

State Bird:
Hermit Thrush

State Flower:
Red Clover

State Flag

State Seal

CANADA

Richford
North Troy
Newport

Swanton
Orleans
Barton

St. Albans
Cold Hollow Mts.
Lowell Mts.
Bluff Mtn.

Fairfield

Ft. Ste. Anne
Grand
Isle
St. Albans Bay

LAKE
CHAMPLAIN
Mallets Bay

Cambridge

GREEN MOUNTAINS

Worcester Mts.

Calvin Coolidge
30th President of
the U.S., 1923-
1929; born at
Plymouth

Fletcher Mtn.
Mt. Mansfield

Winooski
Essex
Junction
Stowe
Burlington
Waterbury
Camels Hump

St. Johnsbury

Hogback Mtn.

Northfield Mts.

★ MONTPELIER

Barre

CONNECTICUT RIVER

Chester A. Arthur
21st President of
the U.S., 1881-
1885; born at
Fairfield

Braintree Mtn.

Middlebury

Bread Loaf
Mtn.

Randolph

Green Mtn.
Nat'l. Forest

NEW HAMPSHIRE

Wilder

White River
Woodstock

Admiral George
Dewey
Naval hero of the
battle of Manila
during the Spanish-
American War of
1898; born at
Montpelier

Rutland
Poultney
Famous
Ice Beds

Plymouth
Constitution
House

Windsor
Ascutney
Mtn.

GREEN MOUNTAINS

Ludlow
Mtn.

Springfield

NEW YORK

Dorset Mtn.
Weston

Bear Mtn.

Bellows Falls

Arlington

North Bennington
Bennington Battle Mon.

Bennington

Brattleboro
Fort Dummer

Ethan Allen
1738-1789, hero
of the American
Revolution and
leader of the
Green Mountain
Boys

MASSACHUSETTS

VERMONT   Capital: Montpelier
Area: 9,609 square miles Rank: 43rd
Population: 389,881   Rank: 47th
Admission Date: March 4, 1791
                                   Rank: 14th

Major Sources of Income:

Manufacturing and Processing
machinery, food products, stone and
clay products, pulp, paper, lumber and
wood products

Agriculture and Livestock
dairy cattle and dairy products, poultry,
maple syrup and sugar products, corn,
potatoes, hay, apples and other fruits

Minerals
stone—marble and granite—asbestos,
talc, slate, sand and gravel

Climate:
Vermont's winters are cold and severe,
with a long season of snow that averages
up to 120 inches in the mountains. Summers are cool and pleasant, with rainfall
of from 35 to 45 inches as an annual
average. The growing season may reach
150 days in the lowlands and along Lake
Champlain, but drops to 100 days in the
mountain regions.

While Vermont is the only New England state not reached by the sea, a large proportion of the state is nevertheless bounded by water. Almost the entire eastern boundary is formed by the Connecticut River; and of the western boundary, big Lake Champlain makes more than half. The large islands in the center of Lake Champlain are part of Vermont.

Between lake and river, Vermont is a long, narrow wedge, three times as wide across the northern boundary as it is at the Massachusetts boundary. Running almost its entire length are the Green Mountains, made up of high ridges often rising 3,000 to 4,000 feet. Mount Mans-. field, in the northwest, is the highest at 4,393 feet. The mountains are heavily forested. The Green Mountain National Forest has two big sections, one in the central part of the state, the other reaching south to the boundary. About a third of the entire area of the state is forested, in spruce, fir, hemlock, white pine, maple, birch, and beech.

Important Whens and Whats in the Making of Vermont

1609   French explorer Samuel de Champlain visits the area and explores the lake which now bears his name.

1724   The first permanent settlement is made at Fort Dummer near today's Brattleboro; New Hampshire governs the region.

1764   The Connecticut River is made the boundary between New Hampshire and New York.

1770-1771   Ethan Allen organizes the Green Mountain Boys to hold territory for Vermont.

1775   The Green Mountain Boys take Fort Ticonderoga and Fort Crown Point in Revolutionary War battles.

1777   Colonists declare their independence, adopt a state constitution, elect a governor and choose the name, Vermont, for their new state.

1791   Vermont ratifies the United States Constitution and enters the Union as the 14th state.

Around Lake Champlain is a narrow, rolling, low plain. East of the mountains, the land drops through a hilly plateau country to the Connecticut Valley.

The Green Mountains are very scenic and offer fine opportunity for hiking, fishing in mountain streams and lakes, hunting, and other outdoor recreation; so they are a favorite vacation area. Their attraction is so great that the tourist business has become Vermont's leading industry. It continues through the winter because of the widespread development of winter sports areas all over the state. The Mount Mansfield area, centered by Stowe, is typical, with many fine ski trails. The ski lifts are used for aerial scenic lifts in the summer.

The Appalachian Trail crosses the Connecticut River and enters Vermont near Norwich, climbs westward to the crest of the Green Mountains, and follows the crest south through the national forest, to cross into Massachusetts. The Long Trail, Vermont's 260-mile trail for hikers, runs with it here but continues north the whole length of the Green Mountains.

Vermont is famous for three products above all others—maple syrup, granite, and marble. The St. Albans, Burlington, and St. Johnsbury areas are leading centers for the harvesting of maple sap and its reduction to syrup and sugar, and the manufacture of candy.

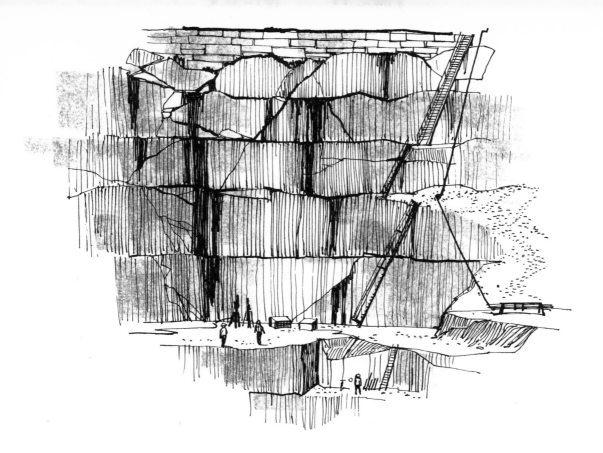

Barre has some of the greatest granite quarries in America, and in the Rutland area the marble quarries recover a great variety of colored marble. These two kinds of stone have been shipped from Vermont all over the world, and appear in many of our famous state and national buildings.

About half the people who live in Vermont are farmers, their farms crowding close along Lake Champlain and the Connecticut River and climbing any hillside not too steep for them. In the lead are dairy farming and poultry raising; hay, grain, potatoes, and apples are also important.

From the days when Ethan Allen and his Green Mountain Boys helped to win independence from England and establish Vermont as a state, Vermonters have been known for their independence. They can turn their hand to doing many kinds of work, and they can take care of themselves in a country of rugged mountains and severe winters. They are a symbol in America of sturdy self-reliance.

Glossary

adze (ădz) a cutting tool differing from an ax in having an arching blade set at right angles to the handle.

beryl (bĕr′ĭl) a salt substance of great hardness, occurring in six-sided crystals, commonly green or bluish green, of which aquamarine and emerald are varieties.

cape (kāp) a point of land jutting out into water; a headland.

channel (chăn′el) 1. the bed where a natural stream of water runs; 2. the deeper part of a river, harbor, etc.

cobalt (kō′bôlt) a tough, shiny, silver-white metal which is somewhat magnetic. It is related to iron and nickel and is found with them.

cog roads (kŏg) roads or paths used by wagons which have cogs on the wheels. A cog is a tooth or spike on the rim of a wheel.

deciduous (dĕ sĭd′ ū ŭs) falling off at maturity, or at certain seasons, as some leaves. Deciduous trees lose their leaves once a year as opposed to evergreens which keep their leaves the entire year, year after year.

drift (drĭft) rock material deposited in one place after having been moved from another.

drumlin (drum′lĭn) an elongated or oval hill of glacial drift.

headland (hĕd′lănd) a cape or high point of land or rock projecting into the sea.

hook (hŏŏk) a piece of land resembling a hook in form, as a narrow cape turned landward at the outer end.

mammoth (măm′ŭth) 1. an elephant no longer living, known by its large teeth and cement-like material between the teeth; 2. referring to size—being very large.

manganese (măng′ga̍ nēs) a grayish-white metal with a reddish tinge which is not magnetic.

mantle (măn′t′l) a covering; something that envelops, enfolds, or covers.

mastodon (măs′tô dŏn) an elephant-like animal which is no longer living, differing from a mammoth in the molar teeth.

migrate (mī′grāt) 1. to move from one country or place to another, with plans of establishing residence; 2. to pass periodically from one region or climate to another for feeding or breeding, as some birds and animals.

moraine (mô̍ rān′) an accumulation or collection of earth, stones, and debris deposited by a glacier, sometimes being over 600 feet high.

notch (nŏch) a deep, close pass, a narrow gorge.

peninsula (pĕn ĭn′sū là) a portion of land nearly surrounded by water and connected with a large piece of land by a neck; also any piece of land jutting out into water.

planetarium (plăn′ė târ′ĭ ŭm) 1. a model or representation of the planetary system which shows the movements of the planets throughout the year; 2. a room or building containing such a model.

plateau (plă to) an elevated expanse of land.

porous (pō′rŭs) full of pores or openings; something which allows the quick absorption or passing through of liquids.

ratify (răt′ĭ fī) to approve or confirm.

secession (sė sĕsh′ŭn) 1. the act, or condition following a withdrawal; 2. the withdrawal of a state from the national Union, as that of eleven states in 1860-61.

siege (sēj) 1. the surrounding of a fortified place by an army to force surrender; 2. a continuing attempt to gain possession.

sinew (sĭn′ū) a tendon; a tough cord.

temperate (tĕm′pēr ĭt) moderate, mild; not hot or cold.

tidewater (tīd′wôt′ēr) water overflowing land at flood tide; also, water affected by the ebb and flow of the tide.

tourmaline (tōōr′mà lĭn) a mineral, usually black, but sometimes blue, red, green, brown, or colorless. When transparent and cut, it makes a gem of great beauty.

tradition (trà dĭsh′ŭn) 1. the passing on of unwritten stories, customs, beliefs, etc.; 2. something handed down from the past to a new generation.

vanadium (và nā′dĭ ŭm) a substance which glows under radiation; a steel-white metal, soft and easily hammered thin.

vulcanize (vŭl′kăn īz) to treat crude rubber or rubber latex chemically to improve its strength, hardness, and elasticity.

Grateful acknowledgment is made to the following for the helpful information and materials furnished by them used in the preparation of this book:

United States Department of the Interior, National Park Service; particularly Acadia National Park and its management.

United States Department of Commerce, Bureau of the Census, Field Services, Chicago, Illinois.

State of Connecticut Development Commission.

Maine Department of Economic Development.

The Commonwealth of Massachusetts Department of Commerce.

New Hampshire State Planning and Development Commission.

Rhode Island Development Council.

State of Vermont Development Commission.

International Visual Educational Services, Inc., Chicago, Illinois.

Index